I need a
man

n. a male person

v. modeling godly
manhood through
mentorship

O. JERMAINE SIMMONS

Scripture quotations are taken from the *Holy Bible, New King James Version*, Copyright © 1982 by Thomas Nelson, Inc. and the *Holy Bible, King James Version. KJV.* Public Domain.

FIRST EDITION

ISBN: 978-0-9976982-9-9

Library of Congress Control Number: 2016954005

Published by

P.O. Box 2839, Apopka, FL 32704

Printed in the United States of America

Dedication

This book is dedicated to the men who have helped shape my life—my paternal grandfather, the late Rev. Dr. Perry Simmons, Sr.; my maternal grandfather, Jimmie L. Griffin; my father, the Rev. Dr. Perry Simmons, Jr.; my uncle, the Rev. Dr. Daniel Simmons; and my pastor, the Rev. Dr. Cameron M. Alexander. These men have had an indelible impact on me as a young man, and as a developing leader. I thank you all for the lessons, the correction, the discipline, and the high standard you set for me throughout the years. This book is dedicated to you. My prayer is that it will impact lives in the way you have influenced mine.

Table of Contents

Introduction

Whenever you hear the phrase "I need a man," it is usually spoken by a woman who is searching for a husband, a boyfriend, or at the very least, a companion for the moment. It speaks to a void that needs to be filled, and only a man will do the trick. A working man preferably, a godly man would be even better. But there are some who have digressed to such a place of loneliness where *any* man will do.

Let me say up front that this is not a book written to help women find a man. (Sorry to disappoint.) I am not offering "tips" on dating, relationships, or any other such topic, at least not in this book. This is, however, a book about manhood, and the importance of men taking our rightful place in the family, in our churches, and in the community at large. We will take a hard look at the state of the world today, and what may be a shortage of active men in many aspects of our society.

By the end of this book, you will come to discover that we all need a man, no matter what age or stage you may be at this moment in time. I believe men have been given a mandate from God to lead and invest in those around us. It is not a knock on women or womanhood. But as you will soon discover, there are certain assignments that God intended for a man to carry out. And my prayer is that we will embrace them with a sense of passion and purpose.

Friends, prepare to be challenged, convicted, empowered, and inspired. I now understand what is missing in many of our lives. We don't need more money. We don't need more degrees. The truth about our world is that we need a man!

CHAPTER 1

What is a Man?

At some point or another, all of us have engaged in some level of discussion about manhood. Everyone has an anecdote or some nugget of wisdom to contribute to the conversation. Books have been written, both sacred and secular. Talk shows have breached the topic, with panels of *experts* weighing in. And from these different mediums, some very powerful ideas were birthed. Men's programs have been created, mentoring initiatives have been put in place. But in lieu of all these wonderful efforts, I feel it best to dig down to the most fundamental question we face in society today. *What is a man?*

This is a very broad question. One that cannot be answered with a simple definition. However, that's exactly where I'd like to start. Let's take it from a secular standpoint, and then move toward a more sacred understanding. A man can be defined as *a human or an adult male belonging to a specific occupation, group, nationality, or other category.* Pretty simple, right? I would venture to say that all of us agree on this secular definition. There's no standard, no filter, no regulating characteristic outside of the fact that in order to be a man, you must be a male of a certain age.

However, when we move toward a more sacred definition, in this case a Biblical point of view, we discover that much more is required for manhood other than being a male of a certain age. While the world may consider you to be a man by the age 18, and in some cultures even younger, there is a Biblical standard that must be applied in order to understand the character and the function of real manhood.

There is something called "The Rule of First Mention." Meaning, in order to comprehend the original context of a word, you have to trace that word all the way back to its Source. Who mentioned it first? What were the circumstances or situations that brought this word about? In this case, we can trace manhood all the way back to God. Yes, God is the Creator and the origin of all life. And according to John 1:3, "all things were made by Him; and without Him was not anything made that was made." That's a simple truth that cannot be overlooked. But let's go deeper.

The first time we see the word "man" is in Genesis 1:26-27, when God says;

> *Let us make man in our image and after our likeness,*
> *and let them have dominion over the fish of the sea, and*
> *over the fowl of the air, and over the cattle, and over all*
> *the earth, and over every creeping thing that creepeth*
> *upon the earth. God created man in His own image, in*

the image of God He created him; male and female He created them.

That word "man" is "adam" in the Hebrew language. It means ruddy, having a red color. This speaks to the truth that man was formed out of the dirt, more specifically the dust of the ground (Genesis 2:7). In another sense, it speaks to mankind in general.

What we see in the verses of first mention is that man had a clear identity and a clear assignment from God. God is his creator, his source, and his boss. He gives Adam a job, an idea which we will explore in greater detail later.

So to put this truth in perspective, a man cannot know who he is outside of God. It doesn't matter how much education, experience, or exposure you have. You cannot know who you are nor can you discover what you were called to do in this world outside of the context of your Creator. We are created male and female. That's identity, and a simple a matter of biology. But Biblically speaking, you can't be the man or woman you were created to be without a right relationship with God.

Those who attempt to define themselves outside of a Biblical context is like trying to understand an iPhone without Steve Jobs' input. He is the god behind the gadget, the creator of the concept. And while you may be able to use the phone and discern the technology, your understanding will always be limited as long as you ignore the original designer.

Is that not what we see in the world today? Mankind has gone about the business of defining itself. Subsequently, when we run into defects or "bugs" in our operating system, we never think to consult the Manufacturer or His Manual. This is dangerous because not all our assumptions are accurate, and not all our solutions are good ones. I see clear evidence of this when I look at who's defining manhood outside the Word of God.

Depending on who you talk to, manhood means different things to different people. Outside the context of being a male of a certain age, I have seen at least three different perspectives expressed by us, mankind. These are the lenses, if you will, through which most people view manhood. And I will break them down individually. We have the Self, the Sisters, and the Society.

Self- this is probably the most dangerous view of manhood. Because depending on how you're wired, your view of self may not be accurate. As Proverbs 21:2 teaches, "every way of man is right in his own eyes..." If you ask me about myself, I would reply that am a flawless and wonderful human being. But on my more honest days, I would have to admit that I am broken, blemished, and full of imperfections. How many of us will actually admit that? Especially as men. Are we able to see the flaws and the character traits that need improvement?

When I get dressed for the day, and I ask my wife how I look, I'm expecting an answer that will reinforce my shallow ego. I want to hear her say "You are perfect and ready to take on the world." Even our 12-year-old son expects us to compliment him on his looks, his outfit, and his odor. Parents know exactly what I mean by this.

Well, the problem is there are times when compliments are not in order. It is an honest critique that we need. If my socks are mismatched, or if my tie is too boisterous for the room I'm about to walk in, if our son has sleep in his eyes or crust on the side of his mouth, this is not the time for ago stroking. This is a time for honest assessment and improvement.

See, if it were up to me, my self-perception says I'm fine. But life will teach you that you can't always rely on yourself as an honest critic. That's where many men fail in life. We only want to see the best in ourselves. So we ignore those things that are wrong or out of place. Now, I don't want to make you feel like a complete disaster. There are plenty good traits and wonderful attributes about you, I'm sure. But the truth of the matter is, your life's socks don't always match. Your life's tie is crooked sometimes. And to keep from having to change it, many men will declare that you like wearing it that way.

This is a sensitive subject to breach with men and even young boys. There is something about the male ego that won't easily accept what appears to be criticism. That's why we built up so many false images of ourselves, and most of it is mental. We tell ourselves that everything is OK, even if the world around us says otherwise. Subsequently, our flaws are not really flaws. Our addictions are not that big of a deal. Our vices aren't really hurting anyone. And our personalities aren't really a problem. We are just misunderstood. Right?

This is why many of us are so argumentative. What we're really doing is warding off any idea that suggests we need to change. After all, it's my tie. It's my outfit. It's my look. It's my life. And as long as my personality works for me, who are you to question my choices or my character?

We see an extreme example of this in Mark 5:1-9. Jesus is met by a man possessed with a demon. And as soon as he encounters Jesus, the evil spirits in him begin to react. Check out verse 7. The spirits in him cried with a loud voice, and said, "What have I to do with thee, Jesus, thou Son of the most high God? I adjure thee by God, that thou torment me not." Friends, this is a man in critical condition!

Understand that when comfortability is met with conviction, when a man is challenged to change, there will always be a struggle within us to remain the way we were. In the case of the demoniac, he was comfortable with his condition. His perception of self was that he was just fine the way he was. Why torment me? Why challenge me to live better and be better? This is the resistance I see in many men, including myself. And whether that challenge comes from our family, our friends, or some spiritual authority figure, you are in for a fight because our self-perception says that I am not the problem. If you are attempting to define yourself based on your tastes, your opinions, or your personal preferences, you, my friend, are in trouble.

Sisters - The previous section dealt with the dangers of men defining themselves. But in a few moments, you will see how even another set of eyes can be inaccurate. Many men have fallen prey to this next group of definers. I'm talking about the ladies. The women in our lives. Our mothers, our sisters, or the female species in general. We all care how the sisters feel about us. As a male, it is quite natural to seek female attention, approval, and affection. But the danger in letting women define your manhood, is that they build it based on *their* desires rather than God's design.

Before I go any further, let me qualify my comments by saying that not all women's opinions are wrong, just like all your self-perceptions are not wrong. However, it is still quite dangerous to allow women to define manhood. If for no other reason than the fact that they've never spent one day as a man. With that being said, let's look at some of the more common descriptors.

Most women will define a man is a provider and a protector. He has means, money, and the mind to get things done. In order to be considered a worthy man, some women have set height requirements, salary minimums, and a skill set that ranges from G.I. Joe to Bob the Builder!

How many talk shows have we seen where women are sitting on a panel discussing men, manhood, or the lack of "good men" available for marrying and mating? If you listen to them, you would think that we have a planet full of women and no men at all. That idea may seem like a stretch. But I exaggerate this point on purpose in order to highlight the error in our thought processes.

Here's the problem with the Sister's logic. If she's only defining manhood based on her needs, then a man will find himself locked into an unrealistic set of expectations. There are plenty of "good men" in the world who don't meet the height requirements nor the salary minimum. Is the sanitation worker not a good man? Is the 5-foot brother not a good man? Is the man who lives in a trailer not worthy of respect and honor? Some women have great expectations. But it's based on a shallow standard to begin with.

At the time this book was written, I have been married for 14 years. And I've been with this wonderful woman long enough to know that the bar never stays the same when it comes to her expectations. Some days I'm the king of the castle. Other days, I'm the thorn in her side. It changes depending on the situation. But if I allow my wife to define my manhood, or even my "husbandhood," I may be in trouble depending on her mood. Hang on ladies, the book gets better.

My point is that you can't totally trust the opinion of a woman to define a man. She's not his creator. She can only pray to diagnose his behavior in any given moment. Manhood is an experience that is foreign to a woman. She can only speculate from a distance. Yes, there are qualities that a man should exhibit that will benefit a woman. But the core of who a man is, and his purpose in life, that cannot be defined by the Sisters.

Where does a Sister's definition come from anyway? Who shapes a woman's perception of what a man is? More than likely it is her own context and experience. Her mother's opinion that was passed on, her experiences or lack thereof with her own father, her previous relationships, even her sibling dynamic with her brothers. These factors, and more, can either help or hinder the understanding that a woman has of a man.

Fellas, if we allow women to define us, we are subject to whatever bar she has set in her own mind. It is not to say that our wives or our sisters can't hold us accountable. But I submit that there must be a standard already set in order for a woman to define and understand manhood. One of the issues we will focus on later is the single mother raising boys. If her definition of manhood is skewed, she will attempt to mold a man in her image and after her likeness. But he will turn out damaged and dysfunctional to say the least.

Society- The perception of Self and the perception of the Sisters can be traced back to the perceptions of society. With the way this world thinks and operates today, society has done a number on gender identity and role definitions. How the Bible defines manhood, society has turned that idea on its head. Society defines manhood by physical appearance, monetary gain, acquisition of power, even his sexual appetite and ability.

Depending on the country of your context, manhood takes on different shades and expressions. Since America is the only country I've ever lived in, I can speak with some authority about how America has manipulated manhood. When you look at the media, and even the world's music, the values we adopt from the Bible are certainly not reinforced. The image of the tough guy, the bold romantic lover, the powerful business mogul, the wealthy king pin who rides through his hood like a hero. These are the images that are constantly being fed to our subconscious self. And if you have nothing to counteract that, you may start to feel inadequate or unaccomplished as a man. Or worse yet, you will try to build a persona based on those parameters.

There may be some of you who think I am overreacting and am being too critical. But remember that the thief's objective is to "steal, kill, and destroy." And his tactics are more subliminal in nature. Let's take the image of fatherhood for example. In the 1950's and 60's, what some would consider the "golden age" of television, we had images of men who were present, intelligent, and responsible. Men like Ward Cleaver (Leave It To Beaver), Ricky Ricardo (I Love Lucy), Sherriff Andy Taylor (The Andy Griffith Show), Steve Douglas (My Three

Sons), and Jim Anderson (Father Knows Best). They were the crust of their community. But more importantly, they were an image of manhood in America. Credit to Google for helping me out with some of those. I'm still a young man.

Then in the 70's, we found a little more diversity in the presentation of manhood and fatherhood on television. Archie Bunker (All In The Family), Mike Brady (The Brady Bunch was a blended family), George Jefferson (The Jeffersons), James Evans (Good Times), Howard Cunningham (Happy Days), and many other I'm sure you could name. How can we forget Fred Sanford? Some were affluent, while others were working class or poor. But the presentation we saw on television is that these fathers were present and accounted for.

The 1980's and 90's, my heyday, is where I believe things started to shift. With America becoming more liberal, and with the free-thinking, flower children of the 60's now in control, we began to see what some would classify as a more realistic view of manhood. But in reality the standard was compromised and the bar was significantly lower. Yes, we had Cliff Huxtable (The Cosby Show), Carl Winslow (Family Matters), and Danny Tanner (Full House). But the 80's and 90's also introduced us to Homer Simpson, Al Bundy, and Peter Griffin. (I admittedly am a fan of Family Guy.)

The image of the strong, present, and morally sound father figure was altered into a side show, a caricature, and shell of his former self. The man who the family once relied upon for leadership is now the butt of every joke. He has a job, but he never makes enough money. He's supposed to be a leader. But his wife insults him at every turn about how dumb he is. He tries to fix things around the house to no avail. He tried to manage things only to be laughed at by his children. This is the image that was subtly presented to us in American media. Although it is disguised behind jokes, the subliminal impact is undeniable.

Society defines us as incompetent in many cases. And the women are introduced as the "fixers," the ones who have to get us "straight." Please understand the position I am taking here. In no way am I suggesting we go back to the golden age of television, because there was little to no diversity in those presentations. However, I want you to see how the power of suggestion is used by the media. And with a generation of children who are locked into a screen for most of their lives, it is imperative that we take a hard look at what society is showing them.

Society says that a man should be tough, a fighter, or even a killer. So the image of Al Capone, Tony Montana, Michael Corleone, and Tony Soprano are now built up as heroes. Remember the days when we would root for Batman to beat The Joker? Well, today we live in a world where the villain is cheered and the hero is seen as "soft."

Growing up in the 80's, I was a hard-core wrestling fan. WWF(E) mostly. But I followed it all. I can remember a time when Hulk Hogan was a clear hero. His whole persona was built around being the all-American man, saying his prayers and eating his vitamins. Andre the Giant was a bad guy. The Iron Sheik and The Big Boss Man were enemies. And no matter who Hulk went up against, the crowd would cheer for him to drop a leg on those bad guys and bring home the title. I hope I'm not losing you with my childhood memories.

What has happened in the last 15 years, there's been a shift in how we view good and evil. My son has taken on my love for wrestling. And with his generation, the heroes are booed and the bad guys are cheered. John Cena gets booed out of every arena he wrestles in, even though he is the 2016 equivalent of what Hulk Hogan was to me. Roman Reigns is even worse. But bad guys like Brock Lesnar or Kevin Owens, they get cheered for beating up the good guys and making them bleed.

My point is that society has shifted its definition of manhood. And we've gone even more to the left in terms of morals and values. A man's sexual conquests are now seen as a badge of honor for us to show off to the world. The idea of commitment and monogamy are almost non-existent. So rather than be Mike Brady, we'd rather be Ron Jeremy. You can research who he is. Or better yet, don't.

The problem with letting society define manhood is that there is no moral filter or code of conduct. Society says do what you want, with no regard of consequences. So while the man who is rich or conquers many women may get a pat on the back from the world, the reality is, he is far from the God-standard. To the millionaire, the accomplished business man, or the popular figure with many followers, all these things are commendable, but it still doesn't define you as a man.

Jesus said in Mark 8:36, "what does it profit a man to gain the whole world and lose his soul?"

So then, if we can't trust society, if we can't trust the sisters, and we can't trust ourselves, who do we go to define manhood? As I stated before, we must go to the Scriptures.

The Law of First Mention teaches that man got both his identity and his assignment from God. He was created in the image and the likeness of God. So the question is not how I view myself. The question is how does *God* view me? I am fully aware of the arguments and disagreements that many people have with the Bible, whether it its authenticity or its applicability in today's culture. But the argument I'm making is not an argument at all. It is a declaration of what Scripture teaches. And I present it without hesitation or insecurity.

Adam was created by God, and "pre-loaded" with a God consciousness. He was given a sense of self only in the context of his relationship with his Creator. He was not a free agent. He was not a wandering creature looking for purpose and fulfillment. Scripture teaches that man became a living soul only after God blew the breath of life into Him.

The point I want to drive home is that you cannot fully know who you are without knowing your heavenly origin. There is a Divine design for your life. There is a predetermined path and plan for your existence. God says in Jeremiah 1:5,

Before I formed thee in the belly I knew thee; and before thou camest forth out of the womb I sanctified thee, and I ordained thee a prophet unto the nations.

This speaks to man's creation and his calling in the world. When we reach the section on parenting, you will understand this truth with greater depth.

To recap, the only way to understand man is to understand his

Manufacturer. A *real man* is one who identifies himself as a created being. A male who knows his Master. Submission to God is key, because in order to be a leader, you must be willing to follow the One who is YOUR leader. The next chapter will dig deeper into this concept.

Who you are is tied to who God is. His will, His ways, His character, and His destiny for you. Now, don't get spooked out by that word *destiny*. I am simply speaking of the plans that God has for each individual He created. As a man, you don't have to wander around wondering what your purpose is in life. If you seek God first, He will give you your assignment, just like He did for Adam.

I can't trust myself. I can't fully trust my sisters. I definitely don't trust society. So I must lean on the Word of God to define me, and the Spirit of God to determine where He has assigned me.

QUESTIONS FOR DISCUSSION

1. What is a man according to God's standard?

_____

_____

_____

_____

2. Have you been negatively influenced or effected by the expectations of others regarding manhood? _____

_____

_____

_____

_____

3. What is your destiny in life? _____

_____

_____

_____

_____

CHAPTER 2

The Man's Assignment

As I previously stated, a man finds both his identity and his assignment from God alone. When God created Adam, He also laid out his assignment in the world. He was to have dominion (leadership) in the earth, which would eventually carry over to his relationship with his family and his community.

I have often found myself in trouble when I've made certain statements about manhood. One such statement is the idea that leadership is male. But before you burn this book or delete it from your device, let me be clear in my assertion. I am not saying that females cannot lead. Women have more than proven their ability to take on and master any task that is presented to them. Today women are heads of households, CEO's of companies, managers of construction sights, military officers, political powerhouses, and even pastors of churches. However, when I say that leadership is male, what I mean is that there are certain things that a man *should* take on, even in lieu of a woman's presence.

For example, if a burglar kicks in my door at three in the morning, I would be less than a man if I look over at my wife and say "dear, you need to go and see what that noise is all about." Her expectation of me as her husband is to investigate that invasion, even if it costs me my life. And rightfully so!

It is not that she is incapable of protecting herself. (My wife is pretty tough.) And there's a good chance the two of us could take an intruder out. But as a man, as the head of my household, something within me says that it is my duty to protect my family. This is what I mean when I say that leadership is male.

I believe there are women who do what they *have* to do from day to day, but not necessarily because they want to. Find me a woman who *wants* to struggle raising children by herself. Find me a woman who is excited about the idea of taking on two jobs to make ends meet. My argument is not against female independence. They've proven their ability to manage without a man. But there's no way I can read the Bible, or even wake up in my man-skin every day, and not acknowledge the fact that God expects me to provide leadership to those around me.

Right about now I can see a group of men cheering me on for that last paragraph. However, fellas, let me be clear on what it means to be the head of the house. And I hope you'll still be cheering by the end of this chapter. To be head of anything means to be accountable for it. Don't imagine a king sitting on a throne being fed grapes by his royal subjects. Imagine a slave being ordered around and paid very little!

As a man, you are accountable for what happens in your household. Whether that be a house of one, or with a woman and children. You are spiritually accountable for the condition of those you've been assigned to. But far too often, we see headship as a title rather than a task. To be pastor of the Jacob Chapel church means that I am the chief servant. It means that I am to sacrifice everything for the good of the congregation. While it is true that Jesus paid the ultimate price for the Church's sins, it is the under-shepherd who must do all he can to protect the sheep.

As men, our assignment is to lead. And that matters all the more when it comes to worship and serving God. In that famous quote from Joshua 24:15, the leader said "as for me and my house, we will serve the Lord." He didn't take a vote in his house. He spoke *for* his house. He wasn't being a dictator. He was being an accountable leader. In essence Joshua said "if nobody else in my house worships, I will worship." That was his stance as the leader.

To be the head means to be responsible. It means to set an example for everyone around you. If nobody else works, a man should work. If nobody else is responsible, a man should be responsible. Before you send your wife or child to answer the door, you should be sure it's safe for them. If you're a husband, this idea is even more critical for us. Because being the man in that relationship, you are expected to sacrifice if nobody else does.

Let's take a quick look at how Paul describes a man's leadership of his wife. Ephesians 5:22-24 is the group of verses men usually start and stop with. It says,

> *Wives, submit yourselves unto your own husbands, as unto the Lord. For the husband is the head of the wife,*

even as Christ is the head of the church: and he is the saviour of the body. Therefore as the church is subject unto Christ, so let the wives be to their own husbands in every thing.

Yes sir! That's our verse! Fall in line, sisters! I am King, and you must submit! But wait, fellas, you have to read on a little further so you won't be guilty of isolating the Scriptures. Verse 25 says,

Husbands, love your wives, even as Christ also loved the church, and gave himself for it; That he might sanctify and cleanse it with the washing of water by the word, That he might present it to himself a glorious church, not having spot, or wrinkle, or any such thing; but that it should be holy and without blemish. So ought men to love their wives as their own bodies. He that loveth his wife loveth himself.

This is the more accurate statement of what leadership is. If loving the Church meant Jesus had to die for her, what does that suggest about husbands today? It means go answer the door. It means stand in front of the enemy and protect your bride. For all the jumping up and down we do about women submitting to us, if we really knew the context, we probably wouldn't holler as loud. Jesus died for the Church. He submitted to the lowest of lows and made the ultimate sacrifice. That is the real meaning of manhood in the family. And it starts with us following God, and our family should follow suit.

As leader of my congregation, I am accountable for what happens at our church, even the things that are not my fault. If ministries are not functional, if bills are not paid, if the needs of the people are not being met, I can't pass that blame on to my deacons or the choir members. My assignment as leader is to be accountable. And although I receive very little credit, you better believe I take all the blame.

Before I leave this issue, I have to answer another question that I am often confronted with in many of my teaching and counselling sessions. Does being the leader mean that everyone has to do what you say no matter what? The answer is no. In fact, being the head often means being able to listen to wise counsel and heed the advice of others. There is no distinction as to who you can get wisdom from. Women, even children, can give insight on an issue.

As the head of your house, you may not be the best mathematician or manager of money. Such is the case in many households. Wives are sometimes better at budgeting (and spending) the money. So even as the "leader," it is wise to listen to someone who can manage or organize the family finances better than you can. It takes absolutely nothing away from a man to let someone else handle the management duties. My brother, it doesn't make you weak, it makes you wise.

The key to this chapter is not to focus on the authority aspect per se. Leadership and headship boils down to accountability. In the end, God will hold the man responsible for the outcome of the family and the community. Keep in mind what happened in Genesis. Eve ate from the tree of the knowledge of good and evil. But sin did not enter the world until Adam ate. And when he attempted to pass the buck and blame the woman, God reminded Adam that *he* was created first, and the directions were given to him. Again, accountability and responsibility.

Now, I know there are those who will argue that my ideas are archaic and old-fashioned. Simmons, you really need to get with the times. But my ideas are not my ideas at all. God's assignment to the man was to lead in worship and sacrifice. I can't tell you the number of women who are either married or live with a man. But when the time comes for worship, those men are at home watching Sports Center or out playing golf.

I submit that a man can't lead if he is unwilling to follow. But a woman will do what she feels is right in spite of a man. No my friend, this is not the pastor's fault, nor is it your wife or girlfriend being rebellious toward you. The fact is, if being in church is right, being out of church must be wrong. So take it upon yourself to be ready for worship even if your family isn't.

In addition to worship, work is also a requirement for men. Here again, Adam was given a garden. And his assignment was to tend to it. That sounds a lot like house work to me! Interestingly enough, God doesn't give Eve any directions about the garden, how to clean it, how to care for it. That was Adam's job. Now before the ladies get too excited, let me be clear that both man and woman should contribute to the chores of the house. And if you have children, you have been blessed with little workers to keep that garden clean at all times.

But back to Adam. He was given a clear job. Which reinforces the truth that a man should work. There is some part of this world that you were given dominion over. No necessarily in a leadership role. But wherever your sphere of influence is, that's your dominion. If you drive a truck, that company and the people you interact with becomes your sphere of influence. If you work in an office, or if you clean that office. No matter where you work, my brother, you have dominion in that arena.

There may be a man reading this book who is currently unemployed. Believe it or not, you are in an even greater position of power. You get to decide where you work! In that regard you are a free agent. God has given you a set of skills that can help make the world a better place. So if you can find a job, as my grandfather would say, you can make a job.

Some of us have been given the spirit of entrepreneurship. Which means you are supposed to go out and create a job for yourself and others. Your purpose in the world is to build on it and improve it. Find a problem and solve it. Create a need and meet it. I mentioned Steve Jobs earlier (pun intended). What would the world be like had he not been given the insight and ability to create such an invention as the Mac and the iPhone? The point is, you have been given your assignment. You just have to pray to God about what that is. Most times your skill set can create a job.

Before we leave this chapter, I cannot talk to you about your occupation without talking about your education. Adam was tasked with naming every animal he encountered. In a modern sense, Adam had to have a pretty extensive vocabulary to come up with a different name for all those different species of creatures. As men, we should seek to achieve the highest standards of education and knowledge building.

Whether it be a GED, a diploma, a collegiate degree or certification, some skill or trade that will make us hirable, a man must arm himself with wisdom and understanding.

QUESTIONS FOR DISCUSSION

1. What is a man's assignment in the family?_____

_____

_____

_____

_____

2. What is a woman's assignment in the family? _____

_____

_____

_____

_____

3. How do we resolve disagreements about our roles in the family and in

the community?_____

_____

_____

_____

_____

CHAPTER 3

The Model for Manhood

So far, we have clearly defined manhood. Not by a worldly or a personal standard, but according to Scripture and the expectations of God. A man is a conscious of his Creator. A man is a leader and a worshipper. A man is both accountable and responsible. Not by his own standard. Not by society's standard. And not by the expectations of a woman.

However, a very real issue arises from this conversation. There are many of you reading this book who have never seen a living example of what I just described. You know what the Bible says, and you've heard about all these male figures in Scripture. But how many of us can say that we've had daily interactions with these kind of people?

Were it not for James Evans or Cliff Huxtable, many African American boys in my generation would have had no image of a positive male figure. I'm not speaking to how many of you may feel about Bill Cosby about the moment. I'm talking about the intentionality with which he portrayed a successful Black doctor, leading a brilliant Black lawyer wife, raising five decent children while taking in a few "strays" along the way. No offense to Olivia and Cousin Pam.

What we see in society and what we read in the Bible is radically different than the men many of us know. To make matters worse, the Bible sets such high expectations. If I lived to be 200 years old, I doubt that I could even achieve the faith and the accomplishments of Abraham. Even as a man of faith, I still have to look around my environment and ask, "Where is my example?" Television and movies aren't good enough. I need a tangible, relatable model to gravitate towards in my daily experience.

There was a phrase that became common when I was a boy. Everyone was going around telling us to "man up." Be a man. Be responsible. Be accountable. The world needs you to man up! That sounds good. And I have no doubt that this is possible. But realistically, how can you expect a boy to *be* a man, when he's never had a model for manhood? I didn't say a message about manhood. I said a model for a man. Not telling me, but showing me. How can I be expected to something when there's no one to show me how?

It's like telling me to fly an airplane, or cook a meal. While it may sound empowering for a boy to hear about his potential, it can actually be quite discouraging to that boy who has never had any examples in his life. *Who's going to show me the ropes? Who have I seen fly a plane successfully in my life? Where is the man who shows me how to cook, based on his own cooking experience? In my daily, real-life interactions, where is the model that I am expected to follow?*

Our community lacks models. Our families suffer because of the lack of generational instruction. The result is a culture that gravitates toward athletes and entertainers. But in the sight of God, the responsibility still lies with parents and community leaders to model what our children should follow. You can't expect someone to be a man when they've never had manhood modeled for them. Many of us take our cues from our fathers, or uncles, or big brothers. That's assuming any of them are present. But if those individuals aren't working under a godly, moral code of behavior, there presence in a child's life will do more harm than good.

Many men will testify that they learned as they went along. Trial and error. Plenty of knee scrapes and head bumps. Nobody ever told them, "this is how you date" or "this is how you treat a woman." "This is how you manage your money" or "this is how you run a household." A lot of us just learned as we went along. And if my conscience is not Christ-centered, it's not safe for me to define myself based on what my environment says is acceptable. How can a man be a husband when "husbandhood" has not been modeled for him? As men we know how to move in with a woman. We know how to court and conquer a woman. We know how to lay with her and put our clothes in the closet. But being a husband is more than forwarding your mail to a woman's address and *shacking up,* as my grandmother calls it. But what exactly is it? How does it look?

It's easy to say, "go be a man." But it's difficult to actually walk in that reality from day to day. The purpose of this chapter is to acknowledge that difficulty. I am not making excuses for us as men. But I must be honest and admit that a lot of our behaviors are tied to ignorance and a lack of examples in our own families and the community.

Back to my favorite shows growing up, what did they all have in common? The presence of a responsible male authority figure. While I am proud to see those images on television, the reality for many of my friends growing up was tragically different. Many of my classmates didn't have a dad like Cliff, or an Uncle Phil to adopt them out of poverty. So the commandment to go out and be a man, it is made all the more difficult when you don't have a model to follow.

As men we must have the proper modelling in order to succeed in life. While it is true that many people succeed without models, you can't deny how many young boys are suffering because of a lack of a positive example. The man in the neighborhood who let you drink and told you dirty jokes, that's not a good model. The relative who showed you pornography, that's not a good model either. The man who sleeps over on weekends but will not commit to marry your mother, this is not the kind of man we want our boys to follow after.

My message to our community is that we can't simply tell a boy to be a man. There must be models of what that looks like and how that works. *What does the leader of a household look like? How do I balance a checkbook and maintain a household?* Even something so simple as hygiene and grooming. That can't be announced as a necessity. It must be taught and modeled. I would know because my 12-year-old has me in his life 24/7 and still struggles with hygiene.

Can you think of any men who were good role models for you? Thank God for them because they helped to mold you into who you are today. For the man who had no models growing up, this may explain why he has not embraced the mandate that his family, society, of even God has placed on him. I am not offering an excuse for negative behaviors. But the truth remains that in order to be a man, you need a man to show you how that's done.

Deuteronomy 11:18-25 lays out a beautiful example of how parents should model godly behavior to their children. God says,

> *Therefore shall ye lay up these my words in your heart and in your soul, and bind them for a sign upon your hand, that they may be as frontlets between your eyes.*
>
> *And ye shall teach them your children, speaking of them when thou sittest in thine house, and when thou walkest by the way, when thou liest down, and when thou risest up.*
>
> *And thou shalt write them upon the door posts of thine house, and upon thy gates:*
>
> *That your days may be multiplied, and the days of your children, in the land which the LORD sware unto your fathers to give them, us the days of heaven upon the earth.*
>
> *For if ye shall diligently keep all these commandments which I command you, to do them, to love the LORD your God, to walk in all his ways, and to cleave unto him;*
>
> *Then will the LORD drive out all these nations from before you, and ye shall possess greater nations and*

mightier than yourselves.

Every place whereon the soles of your feet shall tread shall be yours: from the wilderness and Lebanon, from the river, the river Euphrates, even unto the uttermost sea shall your coast be.

There shall no man be able to stand before you: for the LORD your God shall lay the fear of you and the dread of you upon all the land that ye shall tread upon, as he hath said unto you.

Do you see the pattern of blessings that are tied to parental obedience? God promises to bless our every step if we model Godliness to our children. He didn't say pass on money. He said pass on morals. He didn't say leave them the house. He said teach them holiness. If we model good character and values, there's a promise of generational blessings that will overtake our children.

I am a 4th generation preacher. In a sense, pastoral leadership was modeled for me. Although my father being a pastor does not automatically mean God will call me to that work, it does, however, provide me with a model of men who submitted to God and served Him until their dying day. That can happy in every family no matter what the occupation or income.

QUESTIONS FOR DISCUSSION

1. Did you have the proper models for manhood in your upbringing or young-adult life? _____

_____

_____

_____

_____

2. Do you feel properly equipped for manhood? _____

_____

_____

_____

_____

3. Are you confident enough in your ability to teach your sons or brothers about living a godly life? Why or why not? _____

_____

_____

_____

_____

CHAPTER 4

Men as Mentors

For a number of years, I taught elementary school. Fourth and Fifth grade to be specific. And in all my interactions with children, what I noticed about the boys is that many of them were the man of their house. Yes, at nine or ten years old, these young people were already leaders and caretakers.

Unfortunately, they were the products of broken families, and were being raised by single mothers. And in most cases, they were given the responsibility to watch their younger brothers and sisters because mom was working until nine o'clock at night. As I stated earlier, I take nothing away from the woman as a good provider or parent. But we must be willing to admit that there is a problem when this pattern becomes norm.

Travel back with me to my first few days as a school teacher. I was a hopeful, energetic, 22-year-old, ready to sow seeds of greatness in my students. Well, before I could sow seeds, I was met with a jungle of weeds from day one. Not the children themselves. But all the issues I had to cut through and mow down, just to get to the heart of who they were.

Keep in mind the lack of models I talked about in the previous chapter. Here I am, the first man in these children's lives who wasn't a police officer or drug dealer. I was an authority figure of a different kind. I was a man in a suit, telling them to sit down and be quiet. I was a disruption to what became their normal reality. And for a 10-year-old boy who is the man of his house, I was not an asset, I was a threat to his manhood.

Needless to say, my first few weeks of teaching was a crash course to say the least. What I hoped would be an experience like Gerald Lambeau in *Good Will Hunting*, it ended up being more like Joe Clark in *Lean On Me*. I had desks turned over on me, my life was threatened, I even wrestled a few 10-year-olds and lost. But rather than call a school resource officer to arrest them, I immediately had a sense of what was really going on here. These were not delinquents who needed to be detained. These were boys and girls who needed a man. And the only way I going to win them over was to show them that I care.

Teachers are much more than instructors of Reading, Writing, and Arithmetic. They are nurses, psychiatrists, counsellors, cooks, seamstresses, parole officers, and referees, all in one person. But more importantly, teachers are a form of mentors that we often overlook. They spend more time with our children than we do throughout the course of a day. And the services they provide are not reflected in the paycheck they bring home.

What I often did as a classroom teacher was invite different people from our community to reinforce the values I was trying to teach. Keep in mind I taught public school in Northwest Atlanta, Georgia. So I couldn't open up to the book of Deuteronomy and splash anointing oil all over the children. The best I could do was bring in speakers and other positive people. Lawyers, ministers, athletes, musicians, bankers. Anyone who shared my system of values, I brought them in to speak to my class.

From those interactions, many of my students gravitated toward our visitors. So much so that they became a port of their lives outside the classroom. This is what we call mentoring. Boys in particular need a mentor who may not be a member of their family. I became a mentor by default. I was their teacher. But beyond the hours of instruction, those young men needed a man to spend time with them and model the values I spoke about previously.

Coaches are a great example of mentors in many communities. Mothers do a great job of raising their boys. But that coach often serves as a stern reminder of what will and won't be tolerated in school and at home. I have many friends who are pastors. And part of their mentoring in the community is coaching the peewee football team that their sons play on. To those boys, they now have a man who can hold them accountable. When mom has an issue with him at home, she can now call the coach who has the power to take away playing time or impose some type of safe punishment.

At our church, we have a program that seeks to pair each young man in our congregation with a mentor. We have enough active men where they can take on one or two boys at a time. Mentoring is something that must be done on purpose. We also work along with our local district to train mentors to go into the schools. They are screened, trained, and assigned a young man who will become like a little brother. I am pleased to report that those relationships have made a world of difference in those young men's lives. Mothers and grandmothers are grateful to have that kind of reinforcement and assistance in raising their boys.

On that same note, I would caution anyone who wants to be a mentor or start a mentoring initiative in your community. What our boys need more than anything is commitment and consistency. There have been many programs created in the name of mentoring. And there have been plenty of individuals who use children as political props for a season. I submit that our young people deserve better than a seasonal commitment. They need people who are truly interested in their development even when it's difficult.

I was not the first man to make those students promises. They've seen men come and go in their lives and even in their homes. But what makes a difference is when they see us on a regular basis. They need us to love them and hold them accountable even when it's not convenient. Being a mentor means having desks turned over in your face. Mentoring means being disrespected until you can mow down some of those weeds. Being a man for a child means processing their hurts and discerning their dysfunctions, even when it doesn't seem like you're making any progress at all. But whatever you do, just know that mentoring and being a man for someone is a long-term commitment.

I mentioned the program we have at our church that pairs young boys with men. What I failed to mention was that the most recent appeal I made for men to sign up, there was a woman in her 60's who stood and asked that someone mentor her son who was in his 30's! Yes, a 34-year-old man was in need of a mentor. Or at least his mother sure thought so.

That brings me to the final part of this chapter. Boys are not the only ones who need mentors. The man who's reading this book right now, you need a man too! This is what we call peer mentoring. We need someone we can reach out to who can serve as an accountability partner. Usually it's a man of similar age and similar experience. But in everyman's life, there should be a man who we submit to as a mentor.

Throughout scripture, it reinforces the idea that every man needs a man. Abraham was a model for his sons Isaac and Ishmael. And for future generations, God always made reference to Abraham as a model father of many nations. In addition to the fatherly example, Biblical mentoring has also been highlighted in terms of friendship. Proverbs 27:17 says, "as iron sharpens iron, so a man must sharpen the countenance of his friend."

As much as we love and appreciate women, there are still some issues that a woman can't help a man with. She can't relate and she can't understand a man completely. She can sympathize, and send up a prayer for him. But in terms of embracing his issues, the fact remains that a woman can't assist from a place of experience.

Brothers, look around and ask yourself, *who are my friends? What men do I have in my life who can help sharpen me? Where is the additional set of eyes and ears who are holding me accountable for my words and actions?* Don't be guilty of self-diagnosing like the man in the mirror. We should be prayerful to the Lord for a mentor, and a good friend we can't count on to tell us the truth.

Truthfully, our friends have been known to help us get in as much trouble as we've wanted in the past. But how many of our friends can we trust to give us wise counsel and help us make better decisions? My friend, you need a man. You need a man to hold you accountable. You need a man to correct you without fear. As my pastor would say, you need some people in your life who "ain't scared of you."

Where are the men in your life who can hold you to a higher standard? If you wanted to get drunk, I'm sure there's a man in your life who would assist you in that area. If you wanted to run women or gamble away your paycheck, I'm sure you could find a buddy to take you down that road.

But what about making good choices? Do you have a man you can call when you are weak in your flesh? When you need prayer, when you need a shoulder to cry on, when you need someone to sharpen the iron of your character, who do you have in your life that will shoot straight with you and not care how you respond? Yes, you need a man. But not just any man. You need a man who will guide you in the right direction.

When I read the Bible, I try to examine it in context, while also applying it to my daily experience. One such case is when I look at Jesus' relationship with His disciples. In a real since, Jesus was the man for those 12 men who followed Him. They spent roughly three years together, learning from Him and being corrected by Him. They called Him teacher, and eventually He called them "friend."

Throughout the course of their relationship, being the man for those disciples meant a commitment of time and energy. He understood the fact that they would not come to him as "ready-made" disciples. He was patient enough to wait on their development while He invested in them. He was prepared for Peter's personality. He was prepared James and John's ambitiousness. And ultimately, He was even prepared for Judas' betrayal. Yes, being the man in someone's life is ultimately a privilege, but it can also be a painful one indeed.

When David got caught up in his Bathsheba drama, it was the prophet Nathan who came to him and told him his fault. And as a result, we have a journal entry David makes in Psalm 51:1-12:

Have mercy upon me, O God, according to thy lovingkindness: according unto the multitude of thy tender mercies blot out my transgressions. Wash me thoroughly from mine iniquity, and cleanse me from my sin. For I acknowledge my transgressions: and my sin is ever before me.

Against thee, thee only, have I sinned, and done this evil in thy sight: that thou mightest be justified when thou speakest, and be clear when thou judgest. Behold, I was shapen in iniquity; and in sin did my mother conceive me. Behold, thou desirest truth in the inward parts: and in the hidden part thou shalt make me to know wisdom. Purge me with hyssop, and I shall be clean: wash me, and I shall be whiter than snow.

Make me to hear joy and gladness; that the bones which thou hast broken may rejoice. Hide thy face from my sins, and blot out all mine iniquities. Create in me a clean heart, O God; and renew a right spirit within me. Cast me not away from thy presence; and take not thy holy spirit from me. Restore unto me the joy of thy salvation; and uphold me with thy free spirit.

Now, what we know from 2 Samuel 12:1-13, is that Nathan didn't seek to shame David or air out his dirty laundry. Something was revealed to him in the Spirit, and he took that issue to David in private. Far too many times we take miss the commanded to tell the truth in love. If you truly care about a person and you want to see their life improve, the best thing to do is go to them lovingly and tell them their fault.

When Nathan did this, notice how David responds to the conviction. He didn't unfriend Nathan or block him on social media, so to speak. He didn't lash out and post paragraphs on his wall, accusing Nathan of meddling in his affairs. He didn't fight him or hurl accusations back at him in order to deflect attention from himself. He accepted this correction from another man. And in response, he wrote one of the sincerest Psalms we've ever heard.

Look at how personal he is in his admission. He didn't say Bathsheba sinned. He said *I* have sinned. He didn't excuse his mistakes or accuse anyone else. He simply owned what he did and asked the Lord to have mercy. But it's important to note how his turn-around came about. It all started with a man coming to him in love and telling him the truth in confidence.

Do you have that kind of man? I can honestly say that I have about three or four of those kind of men in my life. Even my wife knows that if she ever had a problem with me, because of my strong personality, one of those three men can be called in as reinforcements. I respect them, and they don't fear me. And most of the time, they can be trusted to give sound advice.

My message to men in this chapter is simple. Even though I serve as a man for so many other men, and even though I'm the one writing the book about manhood, even *I* need a man!

QUESTIONS FOR DISCUSSION

1. Who are the men in your family? Talk about their strengths and weaknesses in general. _____

_____

_____

_____

_____

2. How does it feel when you are confronted with your mistakes? _____

_____

_____

_____

_____

3. What is your response to people who seek to correct you? _____

_____

_____

_____

_____

CHAPTER 5

Why We Need Men

B y now we should be thoroughly convinced that men make a difference. The statistics of fatherless children in America are enough to alarm even the strongest of communities. However, there still may be someone reading this who will argue that the issue is not as critical as I'm making it. But if you look at what happens when men are absent, you will see why modeling and mentoring cannot be ignored.

According to a 2015 report from the National Center for Fathering, there are 20 million children in America who don't have a father present in the home. Of that 20 million, 44 percent of them are being raised in poverty. Ninety percent of the homeless and runaway children come from fatherless homes. Seventy-one percent of adolescent substance abusers come from homes where fathers are absent, along with 80 percent of the children who are in psychiatric hospitals. Children in fatherless homes are twice as likely to commit suicide, while they are nine times more likely to drop out of school.

Why do we need men? Because men, godly men, provide balance and stability in communities overall. I hear the arguments on the other side. Many of you have been raised successfully by single mothers, and have shown no traces of those issues I mentioned before. However, none of us can argue against the need for a woman in the family. Therefore, let us not be so quick to dismiss the need of a man, just because we "gotten by" without one in many cases.

Children were not brought into the world without the contribution of men. It only stands to reason, then, that a man must contribute to the development and safety of that child. Men make the difference. God still expects us to be present and accountable in every aspect of this world around us. Ladies, when I say "I Need a Man," it's not to suggest that you can't survive without one. But if you're seeking a man as your companion, the goal should be for a husband, not just a roommate. And if you're going to allow a man into your child's space, it would behoove you to ensure that this man is a godly influence.

The statistics show what happens when fathers are absent. But I submit that the presence of a bad man is worse than having no man at all. He ends up doing more harm than good. Again, back to my school teaching days. Every Monday morning I would have my students write in a journal, telling me about their weekend. And in 90 percent of my students' writings, there was this character who showed up in all of their experiences. His name was "My Mom's Friend." Yes, it was Mom's friend who took us to the carnival. Mom's friend gave us money to go to the store. Mom's friend spent the night with us. Mom's friend got mad at her about her cell phone ringing. Mom's friend cursed at us and told us to go back to sleep. Mom's friend left and took all his clothes out of the closet. And after a few weeks, Mom had a new friend.

This is not fiction, ladies and gentlemen. This was reality for many of my students. So what do we make of a man who is in and out of the household? It means that the value system in that house is lacking or non-existent. Yes, a man is needed. But we must be willing to set certain standards for who gets to be that man.

Brothers, we don't want to be guilty of dropping in and out of anybody's life. Once a woman falls in love with you, she's hooked. He's making plans to be around for the rest of your life and hers. Once you meet her children, that's a done deal. You are expected to mentor and love them just like their biological father would. Even if the biological parent is active in their lives, you have now taken on that woman. And if you love a woman, you have to love all that comes with her.

We need men who are willing to be examples and mentors to our community. As the apostle Paul said in 1 Corinthians 4:16 "follow me as I follow Christ." With that in mind, I want to shift to a slightly different issue when it comes to men being surrogates for children.

What you are about to read is a portion of a letter written by Paul to a young man by the name of Timothy. This passage in 1 Timothy 1:1-7 is what inspired me to write this book. It says,

Paul, an apostle of Jesus Christ by the will of God, according to the promise of life which is in Christ Jesus, To Timothy, my dearly beloved son: Grace, mercy, and peace, from God the Father and Christ Jesus

our Lord.

I thank God, whom I serve from my forefathers with pure conscience, that without ceasing I have remembrance of thee in my prayers night and day; Greatly desiring to see thee, being mindful of thy tears, that I may be filled with joy; When I call to remembrance the unfeigned faith that is in thee, which dwelt first in thy grandmother Lois, and thy mother Eunice; and I am persuaded that in thee also.

Wherefore I put thee in remembrance that thou stir up the gift of God, which is in thee by the putting on of my hands. For God hath not given us the spirit of fear; but of power, and of love, and of a sound mind.

First and foremost, what stood out to me is how Paul called Timothy a dearly beloved son. Those words can't be taken for granted. If you study Timothy's history, there is one verse in Acts 16:1 that reveals the fact that Timothy was the son of a certain Jewish woman who believed, but his father was Greek. After consulting many Bible commentaries, it is safe to assume, especially because of the "but" conjunction, that Timothy's father was not a believer. This is critical to the 1 Timothy passage.

What we see in context is a young man, being raised by his mother and his grandmother. Their names are Lois and Eunice. And at some point in his life, Paul takes on the responsibility of being the man who would guide Timothy toward his true purpose. Remember I said that the need for a *godly* man is most needed, not just a man in general.

Paul calls Timothy his son, a *dearly beloved son.* We can only imagine what this meant to Timothy, but even more so what it meant to Lois and Eunice. There comes a time in every boy's life where a male influence becomes critically necessary. And to have a godly man like Paul, a leader, a church builder, and a powerful example of God's grace, I believe Timothy hit the spiritual lottery when God placed Paul into his life.

In our culture, there comes a time when boys start "smelling themselves." This is the time around age 10 when they become rebellious and express their desire to lead and exercise authority. By the time I was 10-years-old, I was taller than my mother and very assertive in my tone of voice. And when the time came for me to be corrected, that 5 foot 2 inch woman had no problems getting me in line.

However, my mother often found herself exasperated by my mannish nature. And it took all she had not to kill me. That's where my father came in. There was something about that man's presence that put the fear of God in me. I didn't talk back to him like I talked back to my mother. And he certainly didn't have to tell me to clean my room more than once. Now, it could be that he was 6 foot 6 inches tall and 300 pounds. But even in lieu of his size, the fact is, he was my father. He was the man in the house.

Every boy needs a man to help tighten him up. Our sons tend to get beside themselves and forget that they are the child. And it takes a man to remind the young Simba that Mufasa is still in charge. That's what Paul meant to Lois and Eunice. They had a young man on their hands.

And for Paul to call Timothy his son, that presented a new dynamic of accountability and discipline that was needed in that season of his life.

The Bible never says that Timothy was disrespectful. But God knew that he needed a man. It wasn't suggested that his mother and grandmother were incapable. But in order to stir up Timothy's gifts and bring about God's purpose for his life, those women had to be willing to turn him completely over to Paul for mentoring. In fact, Paul gives credit to them for building a solid foundation of faith in Timothy.

Early on in child's development, it is the mother who does the majority of the nurturing. But when puberty kicks in, when hormones begin to rage, when a boy begins his transition into adult maturity, at that point in his life, he needs a man. He needs someone who isn't intimidated by his masculinity. He needs a man who isn't shy about jacking him up by his collar. I'm not suggesting or advocating any form of child abuse. But it is fact that boys need a man to reinforce his values.

I remember a time when my son was being quite disrespectful to his mother. I believe he was 8-years-old at the time. I could hear his tone, and I could feel her heat from the other room. But before she ended up on an episode of *Law and Order*, I decided to intervene and save my sons life. I said to him, "Son, I'm not going to have you talking to your mother that way. Because before she was your mother, she was my wife. And if you every talk to my wife like that again, I will kill you, and make another little boy who looks just like you."

You should have seen the horror on my child's face. I don't know what shocked him more, the fact that I would kill him, or the fact that I would dare to replace him. Now, let me be clear that I had no intentions of actually killing my child. Although I can't speak with much certainty for my wife. But the point I wanted to highlight is that my boy needed a man to step in when his mother's efforts proved to be futile.

Here's the issue. If my son, who has a mother and a father, can still struggle in that way, imagine what the son of a single mother must be going through. Like Timothy, every young man needs a Paul to help temper some of that testosterone. It can be a big brother, an uncle, a male cousin, or a leader from the community.

But I'm writing this book to let men know that Lois and Eunice need you. There's a Timothy out there who needs a man. The will of God for his life depends on it. Who he is and what his is to become, Paul was used by God to help mold Timothy. And many of our sons needs the same kind of mentoring.

Even though I had my father present in the house for my childhood, I can think of so many men who invested in my success, even into adulthood. The leaders of our boys' ministry at my home church, coaches, musicians, band directors, and teachers. All of them served as the village who helped mold me into the man I am today.

When I left home at age 18, I moved to Atlanta from Newark to attend Morris Brown College. I was a musician, and I loved to play church music. And after a year of floating around from church to church as a gigging organist, I stumbled upon Antioch Baptist Church, where Dr. Cameron M. Alexander was the pastor. I had heard of Antioch and Pastor Alexander. But my purpose for going there was to find a place to use my musical talents.

Sure enough, after the service was over, I rushed to where the pastor was exiting and yelled out to him. Looking back on it, I didn't realize how tacky my approach was. But at the time, as a 19-year-old college kid, I didn't care. Something told me this was my new home. The pastor stopped to engage me briefly. And the only thing I could think to ask him was whether or not he knew my father from New Jersey. He did, and he asked me what I was doing there. I told him I was a student at MBC, and that I was a musician looking for an opportunity. Again, tacky, but honest.

Pastor Alexander set up a time to meet with me. And the rest is history. I joined that church, and was given the opportunity to use my God-given talents. But beyond playing the organ and directing choirs, I received the very thing that I needed most in my life in that season. I needed to a man.

I was away from home, and experiencing a very critical time in my young-adult life. And when my father found out that I had joined that church, he said something that I will never forget. He said "Son, whatever Dr. Alexander tells you to do, you need to do it." It may not seem like much. But for a man to trust another man with molding his son, that speaks volumes to how my father viewed my pastor and how my pastor would deal with me in the future.

A few months after I joined the Antioch Church, I felt like the Lord was calling me to preach the Gospel. And between my father and my pastor, those were the men who prepared me for ministry. And given my age, there was plenty of molding that needed to take place. I had earrings in my ear, a cross around my neck (with Jesus still on it), and a sense of entitlement on my shoulder because of who my daddy was.

I will spare you the gory details by summing things up this way. God used my pastor to be the man I needed at that point in my development. He trained me, corrected me, drilled me, disciplined me, and loved me like a son. And when I called home to complain about my hurt feelings, my father reminded me of what he told me when I first joined.

I needed a man, and now I had two of them. And there is no way I would be who I am today had it not been for that Paul and Timothy dynamic. Even today my pastor serves as a surrogate. He has never tried to replace my father. And my father has never been bothered by my relationship with my pastor. These men worked in harmony to usher in God's plan for me. And now, with the men that are in my sphere of influence, I owe it to them to reinvest what was given to me.

QUESTIONS FOR DISCUSSION

1. Who do you have in your life to correct you without fear? _____

_____

_____

_____

_____

2. What gifts did you discover as a result of being mentored?_____

_____

_____

_____

_____

3. Think about the season of your life when you realized your calling or assignment. Who helped you? _____

_____

_____

_____

_____

CHAPTER 6

Mama's Boys

Remember when I said that the Sisters can't be trusted to define manhood? Well, that previous chapter about Lois and Eunice needs a little more expounding. When I look at the dynamic between mothers and their sons, often times I've seen how the child can easily be turned into a boyfriend or a husband. Follow me down this uncomfortable road.

I've observe many a single mother who labels her son as "my little man" from birth. It seems innocent enough. But the language gets more problematic as time goes on. We see internet posts of mothers and their sons with the caption "my boo" or "my handsome little husband." When he gets to be a teenager, those words sounds even creepier. It is not to suggest that these mothers have any sexual feelings toward their sons. But remember, that boy was never meant to be your companion. He was given to you as an assignment.

You don't correct your companion. You don't discipline and take things away from your companion. So when I see a mother giving her son everything he wants and allows him to act like the man of the house, you are disrupting God's purpose for you in his life. You are not his wife. You are his mother.

The danger in making your son into your little husband, is that he will never be able to function is his own legitimate relationships. Mom won't let him date, because "all he needs is me." He won't even become a husband because no one is good enough to marry your little boy. Well, the problem is, your little boy is 27 years old now. And he has yet to learn how to function in a mature adult relationship.

I know it gets lonely as a single parent. But your son is not meant to fill that void. That's why the Bible says that a man should leave his father and mother and cleave to his own wife. He must learn to be the man of his own house. And that requires him to cut the emotional cords of his mother. How ironic is it that the umbilical cord was meant to feed the child in the womb. But figuratively, as adults, women keep their sons tied up so *they* can feel complete! Please don't take my words as being insensitive to your plight. But understand that a young boy needs love and discipline. And you can't give it to him by treating him like your husband.

You can't run his life into manhood. And even when he makes bad choices, it's not always good for a mother to go running after a male child. When I would fall and skin my knee, I knew my mother would be there to pick me up. But my father, he understood the need for self-sufficiency. So there would be times when he would let me stay on the ground, until I realized how to pick myself up, dry my tears, and move on. Children need both compassion and discipline. And a parent has to know when and which one to implement.

Mom, your son needs a man. And it doesn't have to be a man that you are dating. Look in your church, your child's school, or some member of your family or community to find a mentor for your son. There is a biological imbalance that comes from boys who don't have a man in their lives. It is not to say that they won't be successful. But even godly women like Lois and Eunice understood that Timothy needed more than a woman's touch.

Boy Scouts, sports teams, band, martial arts, or any other kind of activity can help boys understand who they are becoming and their place in the world. It takes nothing from you as a parent to admit that your son needs a man.

QUESTIONS FOR DISCUSSION

1. What are the benefits and the disadvantages of being raised by a single mother? _____

_____

_____

_____

2. What does a boy miss out on because of the absence of a man in his life? _____

_____

_____

_____

3. How can we improve the statistics of single parenthood in America?

_____

_____

_____

4. What advice can you give to a woman who is struggling to raise a male child on her own?_____

_____

_____

CHAPTER 7

When Men Get Together

I cannot stress to you enough how much men need other. The principle of iron sharpening iron, there is great value in the right kind of men getting together. In society, we see gatherings of men on many different levels. Men get together to watch sporting events. We meet up to play cards or some other recreational activity. Men drink together, hang out at clubs and bars together, hiking, camping, and even skydiving together.

Whether you consider these activities to be positive or negative, the fact remains that men need to spend time with each other. There is a kindred spirit, and familiar energy when men get together. Unfortunately, there are some men who aren't totally comfortable being around other men. Maybe because of their family dynamic growing up, or because they feel like women are easier to get along with. Some women actually feel this way about being around their kind as well.

But my prayer is that men will be able to come together and

invest in each other. Once you open up to a fellow brother, these can be relationships that can last for the rest of your life. My best friend of over 30 years is a man, of course. And even though there was a season where we lost touch and didn't communicate consistently, it didn't take much for us to reconnect and get things back on track. It was like no time had passed. And we were able to reminisce about the good old days, and pray for even better days in the future.

As a man, I need other men who can help sharpen me. I'm not talking about a man who helps me get into trouble. I'm talking about a man like Jonathan who looked out for David's well-being. Jonathan was Saul's son. And many of you know that Saul was the kind of Israel who developed a passionate dislike for David. The Bible says that he tried to kill David on more than one occasion.

But according to 1 Samuel 19:1-7, Jonathan was the middle man who negotiated to save David's life, at least for a season.

Saul spake to Jonathan his son, and to all his servants, that they should kill David. But Jonathan Saul's son delighted much in David: and Jonathan told David, saying, Saul my father seeketh to kill thee: now therefore, I pray thee, take heed to thyself until the morning, and abide in a secret place, and hide thyself: And I will go out and stand beside my father in the field where thou art, and I will commune with my father of thee; and what I see, that I will tell thee.

And Jonathan spake good of David unto Saul his

father, and said unto him, Let not the king sin against his servant, against David; because he hath not sinned against thee, and because his works have been to thee-ward very good: For he did put his life in his hand, and slew the Philistine, and the LORD wrought a great salvation for all Israel: thou sawest it, and didst rejoice: wherefore then wilt thou sin against innocent blood, to slay David without a cause?

And Saul hearkened unto the voice of Jonathan: and Saul sware, As the LORD liveth, he shall not be slain. And Jonathan called David, and Jonathan shewed him all those things. And Jonathan brought David to Saul, and he was in his presence, as in times past.

That's the kind of man I need! Jonathan loved David so much that he stepped in front of his father's wrath to plead for his life. Do you have friends who will stick by you even when it's not popular to do so? Is there a Jonathan in your life who will risk his own neck to save yours? There is no honor in convenient friendships. And there are very few people you can count on to stand with you in difficult times. But when you find Jonathan, hold on to him.

Think about the chemistry of a sports team. The teams that are most successful are the ones who appreciate each other's gifts and are not intimidated by another person being celebrated. The San Antonio Spurs are a good example of this. Since 1997 they have at least been in the conversation for the NBA championship.

David Robinson was getting ready to retire. And the Spurs had just experienced the worst season in team history. But when they drafted the number one pick out of Wake Forest the following year, Tim Duncan, they immediately became contenders for the title. What's more powerful is how David mentored young Tim. He was humble, teachable, and willing to listen to an experienced veteran.

On the other end, David Robinson was not intimidated by the young man's abilities. He saw them as assets to help the team thrive. With those two big men and a point guard named Avery Johnson, the Spurs won their first championship in 1999.

Since that time, Tim Duncan has continued in the spirit of David Robinson. From one night to the next, anyone could be the superstar of that team. Some nights it's Tony Parker. Other nights it may be Manu Ginobili. But the reason why the Spurs are successful, is because they've bought into Coach Greg Popovich's philosophy that we do better when we work together and put aside our personal need for glory.

One of the reason why the Lakers imploded in the early 2000's is because two men, Kobe Bryant and Shaquille O'Neil could no longer co-exist. They were men, two alpha dogs with dominant personalities. And neither of them were willing to humble themselves long enough for the other to shine.

Whose team is it? Is it Kobe's team or Shaq's team? Those were the questions that were raised in the media every night they played. And even after winning three straight championships together, they still couldn't see the error in their attitudes. They both have admitted this in recent interviews.

If I were Coach Phil Jackson, I would have announced that this is *my* team. Players have to learn to follow the coach. And coaches have to know how to get the best out of players. That is how I view my role as pastor of our church. I announced to everyone in attendance that Jesus is the owner, and we must all embrace our roles.

I constantly pray for ways for men to get together and fellowship. I want our men's ministry, which we call "The Huddle" to be the most active and powerful force our community has ever seen. I am not the kind of leader that has to announce my superiority. We are clear on our roles, and mine is to be the chief servant.

This may be helpful for pastors who want to galvanize the men of your church. Remember, men our naturally suspicious and defensive in a lot of ways. So you have to disarm them by letting you know that you love them, and that you value what they bring to the table.

I am not the head of your house, brother, you are! My job is to coach you and surround you with other men who can strengthen your walk with God and make you a sharper husband and father. You don't have to dumb down to be on our team. Bring your brains and your abilities, and be willing to submit to the Owner. I don't need to step on your neck and make you bow down to me. My position as coach is secure. And more importantly, I celebrate what you bring to this team.

When men get together, there's no stopping us. When we put aside or petty differences and trust each other, we are a spiritual force to be reckoned with. But men have to be willing to submit to authority. Just as I submitted to my father and my pastor, every man must be willing to fall under spiritual subjection.

Psalm 133 says, "Behold, how good and how pleasant it is for brethren to dwell together in unity! It is like the precious ointment upon the head, that ran down upon the beard, even Aaron's beard: that went down to the skirts of his garments." Remember, Moses was the leader for the children of Israel. But Aaron, was his second in command. Psalm 133 describes this ointment, or an anointing as some would call it. It came from God, and poured out to Moses, the leader. But eventually it ran down to Aaron who represented the beard under the head.

I spent a great deal of time telling you about how I submitted to my pastor, my spiritual leader. And I am blessed today because I obeyed even when I didn't want to. I can't tell you the number of times I went to my car and cried or went home and complained because of how I felt I was being treated. But the blessings I've received in the last 20 years, I am so grateful that I didn't run away when I was convicted.

I challenge every man reading this book to connect with a Bible-based church. God will use that pastor to feed you and lead you toward God's will for your life. Maybe you had a bad experience with churches or with pastors. But my prayer is that you will heal from that and be able to trust again.

No person can grow in isolation. Which is why Hebrews 10:24-25 teaches us to "consider one another to provoke unto love and to good works: Not forsaking the assembling of ourselves together, as the manner of some is; but exhorting one another: and so much the more, as ye see the day approaching."

There is a day coming when you will need someone to lean on. And a man who is not spiritually connected will not be able to stand nor will he be able to lead. You need the gathering of believers in worship. You need the fellowship of believers in ministry. There are many things you can do by yourself. But fellowship requires unity with like-minded people.

One year I came back to New Jersey to visit my father. And he summoned me to the kitchen one morning to help him prepare breakfast. Now, before you laugh, anyone who knows me can testify that my breakfast is the best in the world. Now back to my story.

The grits are already boiling. And the meat is being prepped for the frying pan. But the lesson I was about to get on this day was all about homemade biscuits. These aren't canned biscuits, or frozen biscuits in a plastic bag. These biscuits are from scratch, made from whatever my father put in them. But my lesson was in the pan.

He said, "I want you to make a lump of dough and place it in the pan, one after the other." Simple enough for me to handle, I thought. So I went about placing the biscuits a few inches part in the greased pan, and got ready to place them in the oven. My father's reaction would make you think that I was burning the house down. "What are you doing?! That's not how you make biscuits!" And when I asked him to explain, he lit up light a preacher on Sunday morning.

He said "You put those biscuits too far apart in the pan. They have to be closer together in order to cook properly. The heat from one helps to cook the others. And they all rise together!" If I wasn't a broke college student I would have given him an offering. It immediately made sense.

Using my logic and my personality, the biscuits didn't need to be that close to each other. I'm an introvert. I like to stay to myself. So

I figured the biscuits would appreciate being left alone just like me. But the lesson from my father's kitchen is the same lesson God wants to teach us as a community. You can't be that biscuit who sits over in the corner not talking to anyone. You have to be willing to get close to other people. And when you do, we all rise together!

That's the benefit of men getting together. We are all biscuits in a pan trying to rise to our potential. 1 Corinthians 12:26 says that when "one member suffers, all the members suffer with it; or if one member be honoured, all the members rejoice with it." Men need other men to encourage them and help them to rise. When we cry, we need someone to cry with us. And when we rejoice, we need people who aren't jealous and can rejoice with us.

Whether it's a sports team, a church ministry, or a pan of homemade biscuits, the words of the old saints ring true. When all God's children get together, what a time that will be!

QUESTIONS FOR DISCUSSION

1. How often do you get together with other men socially? _____

_____

_____

_____

2. What kind of spiritual gatherings do you attend that have helped you

to grow? _____

_____

_____

_____

3. Why do men take issue with the idea of submission? _____

_____

_____

_____

4. Is crying still seen as a sign of weakness in men? _____

_____

_____

_____

CHAPTER 8

Marches and Movements

I can remember being a teenager in 1995, when Minister Louis Farrakhan organized the Million Man March. I did not attend, nor did any men I was related to. But I can remember the buzz and even the controversy that surrounded that event. Men from every walk of life, every age and stage, every religion and personal creed, they traveled from every corner of America to gather at our Nation's capital.

I watched and listened as men spoke about family accountability. Fathers were there with their sons. And complete strangers stood hand in hand in a spirit of unity. I was only 16 at the time. But even then I felt like something significant was happening in America. There were dozens of speakers, both from the sacred and the secular point of view. Minister Farrakhan being the organizer, he served as the highlight speaker of the event.

Tears were shed, songs were sung. And men left there feeling like they could take on the world for the better. Some 20 years later, I am still proud of what happened at the Million Man March. However, I believe there was something missing. One issue that was not clearly addressed. What happens after the march?

When those men and their sons leave Washington, what happens when they go home? What do those husbands do when they finish crying on each other's shoulders? What do those young men do when they step back into their reality? Herein lies my discomfort. While marches and allies have their place in society, no change can ever occur unless the march turns into a movement.

While the men have clearly been inspired and uplifted, what tools have they been given to build a mini-movement in their neighborhoods, or even their homes for that matter? I believe we have to march into our communities and implement some real ideas. But even when we attempt to do that, we can't embrace our assignment unless we are clear on our identity.

This is where the conversation gets to be uncomfortable for people who are shaky in their faith. Because I stated earlier that a man can't know who he truly is outside of his relationship with God. At the point, the generic message of "we need to do better" is not sufficient. The rallying cry for men to be accountable is not good enough to satisfy God's standard for holiness.

We have to be willing to confront the reality that an unsaved man is no good to his family nor his community. There next march he needs to attend is down the aisle of someone's House of Worship. How can he be a man if he doesn't read the Master's Manual? And how can he benefit his community if he does not know his Creator? When we march into our schools for PTA meeting, the teachers will know that we are actively engaged in our children's education. We are not distant bystanders. We are not occasional observers who make appearances at graduations or promotions. We are men, and we are here!

In the 12 years of my son's life, there has never been a time when I was not present and engaged. However, there are still times when his school administrators and teachers have expressed "shock" when they see both of his parents at various events. It's almost like they saw a unicorn. As if to suggest that my presence is a rarity, and they better capture this moment before I disappear again.

Instead of taking offense to their posture, I had to understand where these administrators were coming from. So often, what they find is a single mother struggling to get their child to school on time. She can't always make the meetings and events because she has to work. There is no man to pinch hit or share in the duties. So when they do see a man, they want to sign you up for every committee and grab a donation from you too! My prayer is that we will become more of a mainstay in our children's schools. That's when the march turns into a movement.

When you are dealing with an impoverished community, bad things tend to happen at a larger scale than most other communities. While it is true that tragedies happen everywhere, we must be honest and admit that when America catches a cold, poor communities catch malaria! Wealth inequality, police brutality, black-on-black crime, these are all issues that make us want to protest.

As I stated before, marches have their place in society. I would venture to say that we would not be where we are as an evolving country were it not for the many marchers and demonstrators who sacrificed for our freedoms. However, I also believe in being proactive rather than reactive. In other words, certain issues would not confront our communities if men would engage in our children's lives on a regular basis.

Where is the man who can be accountable for the women and children who are living in poverty? Where are the men who can mentor the child who has anger issues? Remember the fact that poverty breeds crime. And crime leads to incarceration. So the issue that we clearly see in our communities, and the issues that feed into this pipeline to prison, where are the men who see it as our duty to put a stop to the madness?

We need more than a march when someone dies senselessly. We need more than a protest when police officers go rogue. We need a movement, a commitment from our men to be present, engaged, and accountable. I agree that it won't solve every issue nor prevent every tragedy. But I do believe it will decrease the numbers because the presence of men, godly men, it makes a difference.

QUESTIONS FOR DISCUSSION

1. Do you believe that marches and demonstrations are effective tools for impacting your community? _____

_____

_____

_____

_____

2. What are some of the issues you believe to be vital in your community?

_____

_____

_____

_____

3. What community initiatives are you currently involved with that speak to the plight of men or boys? _____

_____

_____

_____

_____

CHAPTER 9

Men and Ministry

In the last chapter, I applauded the many efforts that seek to bring attention to the plight of our communities. The Million Man March was an awesome demonstration of what can happen when men get together. However, there is a sense of momentary engagement when it comes to marches. There must be something for men to connect to once they march back into their cities. That is where I believe ministry becomes necessary.

Ministry is not just a Sunday morning activity. It begins with worship. But it carries over into our daily existence. Every church that has men or boys should have a men's ministry. I am defining ministry as an active group of believers from a specific demographic who provide teaching, fellowship, and guidance through the various issues that affect the target group.

That may sound complicated, but it's all in there. Ministry should be designed with a specific demographic in mind—Women, Youth,

Young Adults, Singles, Married Couples, and in our case, Men.

Men need to be linked to a consistent program that engages them on a daily, weekly, or at the very least, monthly basis. Ministry is different from worship. Men need a safe space where they can engage in fellowship, dialogue, and prayer. Where can I go when my marriage is in trouble? Who do I go to when my son is acting out of character? Where do I turn when my vices are beginning to pull at me? I need a man. And men's ministry becomes my safe haven for strength and godly support.

Do you know why Alcoholics Anonymous meetings are being held every day? It is because AA understands that no one struggling with that vice can make it alone. Some days an alcoholic is strong. Other days the temptation to drink gets the best of them. But rather than sit at home and summon up my will power, the meeting gives me a support group of people who can relate to my struggle. How many of us can be honest and admit that our will power isn't always strong enough to tame our flesh issues?

That's why I need ministry. That's why I need a men's ministry. It surrounds me with a group of like-minded people who can give and receive support for our various issues in life. One of the tricks of the enemy is to isolate you in your struggle. If the devil can get you to stay home with the blinds closed and curtains drawn, if he can get you by yourself, there's a greater chance he can concur you.

When I'm alone with my thoughts, when I'm isolated in my issue, the only voice I'm hearing is the voice of my insecurities. That's when depression sets in. That's when I feel the need to self-diagnose and self-medicate. Men's ministry allows me a safe space to lay my burdens down. And what I discover when I get amongst other men, is that I'm not the only one who struggles in certain areas.

I can talk to a married man of 40 years, and I discover that what I'm going through after 14 years is nothing new. As men share, and as we allow ourselves to be transparent, we find a commonality with people who hurt just like we hurt. So in reality, you are not the only one who has been to jail. You are not the only one who has made some mistakes in life. You are not the only one who is struggling with the mother of your children. What I thought was just an isolated issue for me, I find that there are men who share my fears, but most importantly, my faith.

Remember, the biscuits can't rise by themselves. The enemy seeks to isolate us to keep us from fellowshipping with other biscuits. Men's ministry is that pan for biscuits. And the church is the oven that gives us heat to rise. I cannot tell you the number of men who have come out of their struggles because of the support ministry. And the miraculous part about it is that no one ever knew that they were struggling. In other words, you don't have to beat a confession out of a man, or force him to spill his secrets in a ministry meeting. All he needs is to be in that environment. The Holy Spirit works miracles when men get together.

Mark Chapter 2 speaks of a man who was in need of some help. He was paralyzed and could not walk on his own. The verses you are about to read speak directly to what I believe men's ministry should be all about. Let's read through them, and then make application to our current context.

And again he (Jesus) entered into Capernaum, after some days; and it was noised that he was in the house. And straightway many were gathered together, insomuch that there was no room to receive them, no, not so much as about the door: and he preached the word unto them. And they come unto him, bringing one sick of the palsy, which was borne of four.

And when they could not come nigh unto him for the press, they uncovered the roof where he was: and when they had broken it up, they let down the bed wherein the sick of the palsy lay. When Jesus saw their faith, he said unto the sick of the palsy, Son, thy sins be forgiven thee.

Imagine this man crippled and lying on a bed. He was unable to walk nor was he able to care for himself. When word got out that Jesus was in town, thousands of people made their way to the house where he was. Notice how the Bible says that Jesus preached the Word unto them. Healing was not His primary goal. He understood the power of ministry over miracles.

So the story goes on to say that there was no more room in the house. And this crippled man couldn't have gotten in anyway. He couldn't walk. He couldn't get himself to the meeting. But what did he have going for him is a few good friends who didn't mind carrying him. He had some men!

When this crippled brother found himself unable to walk, he had some men in his life who were willing to carry him. When they arrived to the house and saw that there was no room at the entrance, these men became even more determined, and they tore the roof off! Yes, they literally raised this man up in his bed, tore the roof off someone else's house, and lowered their friend down to where Jesus was.

Again, let the visual of this scene sink into your mind. The crippled man is laying on a bed, a stretcher if you will. And in order to get him to Jesus, each of his friends had to carry a corner. They became the EMT's for their brother. And they didn't let an obstacle stop them from helping their brother. They did whatever it took to help him. That's what men's ministry should be!

I need men who can help carry me when I can't walk for myself. Don't take me to a club. Don't take me to a bar. Take me to Jesus! Take me to the one who can forgive me of my sins. Because if all I want is healing for my crippled legs, if I'm still a sinner, I'll walk right back into the situation that crippled me. Hear me brothers, salvation is more important than healing. An alcoholic needs to be saved. A drug addict needs to be saved. A sexual deviant needs to be saved. An angry and aggressive man needs to be saved. Why, because if you get his soul saved, if you can get him to Jesus, God works on men from the inside out. His desire is that we walk out of that room saved, not just healed.

Yes, as a healed man, that brother can get up and get a job. But if he is not saved, he'll have a job but he won't have joy. Yes, a healed man can provide for his family. But if that man is not saved, he still won't be able to lead his family.

Men's ministry is the bed I lay on. And there has to be some men in my life who can get me to Jesus. Pray for me. Support me. Encourage me. Teach me. Correct me. These things happen in the midst of a men's ministry gathering. I encourage every pastor to start these kind of initiatives. We have to go after men on purpose. Too many of us are crippled spiritually and can't walk upright. If every man reading this book would commit to carrying a corner for your brother, there's no limit to the number of lives we an impact.

There is another passage of Scripture that talks about men's ministry. But it serves as a source of conviction for those who don't like to get their hands dirty. Remember the demon possessed man I talked about in Chapter 1? There's a simple principle that I need to mention in the context of ministry.

Many times, we who are leaders of churches or participants in ministry, we forget the fact that ministry is designed for people. Human beings, no robots, are the target of our efforts. Many times, our efforts won't be met with gratitude or appreciation. In fact, the demon possessed man was offended by Jesus' presence. It was a confrontation of a spiritual nature.

Here's the point we need to grasp about ministry. If ministry is for people, we must be willing to meet people wherever they are. Literally. You cannot stop the violence in your community if you are not willing to engage violent people. Do we actually talk to gang bangers and drug pushers? Do we actually converse with them like Jesus did the demoniac? I've seen us hold press conferences at the community center. But where are the people who actually engage the demographic they claim to want to save?

The Jacob Chapel congregation is a very diverse one to say the least. I am always prayerful about the racial divide in churches today. But the diversity that I'm speaking of is more of a demographic nature. We literally have everyone in our church, from the GED to the

PHD. College presidents and people on parole. Sheriff's deputies and ex-convicts, doctors and dope addicts. Everyone is connected to the ministry and Master.

Here again lies the issue. If we are not willing to deal with those kind of people, the less desirables, how can we claim that we are doing ministry? I can tell you from firsthand experience that people bring their issues to church every Sunday. When it comes to outreach or community ministry, we have to be prepared for what we will see when we step outside our doors.

You can't help the issue if you won't go near the individual. We can't minister to addiction if we're afraid to touch addicts. Literally. We can't minister to poverty if we refuse to be around homeless and hungry people. No one comes to Jesus ready-made. We don't come already cleaned up and ready to serve Him. He meets us where we are and grows us into the people He wants us to be. That process takes time. But it starts with a group of men who aren't intimidated by people's issues.

QUESTIONS FOR DISCUSSION

1. Are you comfortable around other men? If not, please explain why.

_____

_____

_____

_____

2. What are some ways we can create a more inviting environment for men in our churches or community groups?_____

_____

_____

_____

_____

3. What is the major issue that you find most difficult to discuss?

_____

_____

_____

_____

CHAPTER 10

Giving Back

A few chapters back, we spent a great deal of time talking about the dynamic between Paul and Timothy. He was the seasoned man for that young man. He was the surrogated who stepped to the plate for Lois and Eunice. Have we ever stopped to ask why that is? Why would Paul take the time to mentor a young man?

Some would say that he was investing in the next generation. Maybe he mentored Timothy to ensure that the Gospel ministry would continue beyond his own administration. While either of those things may be true, here's why I believe Paul mentored Timothy. Because somebody mentored him!

Those of us who are familiar with Scripture know that Paul was not always Paul. In fact, he started out as Saul from Tarsus. He was not a Christian, he was a killer. He was not a minister, he was a menace to society. Acts chapter 9 speaks of a day when Saul was on his way to Damascus. He had already written letters to all the Christians in town, letting them know that their days were numbered.

As a religious zealot, Saul felt that it was his duty to purge every believer from the face of the earth. Killing them was his mission in life. From his school of thought, he was doing the world a favor by stopping this new movement called Christianity.

That's where he was met on the Damascus road by a bright shining light. The light was so intense that it blinded him and knocked him off his beast. All of a sudden, he heard a voice crying out to him saying, "Saul, Saul, why are you persecuting me?" He inquired about this voice he was hearing. "Who are you, Lord?" The voice said, "I am Jesus, the One you are persecuting."

From that point on Saul is spooked out of his mind. He doesn't know what to do with himself. He has been convicted and confronted at the very point of his sin. And it took the voice of Jesus to compel Saul to make a change. Understand that a man nor a ministry can help a person see the error of their ways. There must be an inner conviction and a spiritual experience that moves a man from a sinner to a saint.

Jesus told Saul to rise up and make his way into the city, and await further instructions. But in the meantime, God had already spoken to a man named Ananias about Saul. And he would be the man who ministered to this blinded soul in transition. Jesus told Ananias to make his way to a street called Straight. (You gotta love the irony in that.) And he was to enquire about a man named Saul who is praying and waiting for help.

I can appreciate the transparency that the Bible uses at this point. Because Ananias wasn't exactly thrilled about this meeting with Saul.

Saul the killer? Saul the murderer? Saul who just sent us letters last week threatening to murder us? Jesus meant exactly that! You, Ananias, are to be the man for a brother who could potentially take your life!

Listen to what Jesus says to Ananias in verses 15 and 16. He says, "Go thy way: for he is a chosen vessel unto me, to bear my name before the Gentiles, and kings, and the children of Israel: For I will show him how great things he must suffer for my name's sake."

God had a plan for Saul. But Ananias would be the man who helped him in the transition. Paul was not yet Paul. But God saw the potential in spite of his plight. How many of us can remember a person who helped us when we were in our Saul stages? Ananias had to be reassured by God himself, because "Saul's" are not always the easiest people to minister to. He's rough around the edges. He's got anger issues and a killer personality.

Thank God for people like Ananias! He was willing to trust what the Lord told him, even though Saul showed no initial signs of spiritual progress. The "thug" you meet on the streets, God has a plan for him too. The high school dropout, the drug dealer, the pimp, the gang member, or the abusive husband, God can turn a thug into a theologian!

What we need is a group of saved men who aren't afraid to engage these Saul types. We see them every day. But we avoid them because they require more work than the average soul. Ananias spent 3 years working with Saul along with other saints. I have to believe that the majority of them were men.

Often times we breeze through these stories in the Bible. So there may be some of you who thought Saul got converted over the course of a few days. That was not the case. It took years for Saul to become Paul. He didn't preach a sermon a week after he was called. He didn't attempt start a ministry fresh off the Damascus road. Let this be a warning for those who feel a call to the preaching ministry. Saul was not given a platform until he spent years with a few good men.

The Paul we see today is not the man we knew initially. For those of us who want to see lives changed, understand that is a long-term commitment. Ananias was inconvenienced by this assignment, I'm sure. And he had to endure the ridicule of some people in community for dealing with Saul in the first place.

Our church has often been criticized for the kind of people who attend. "That's the church where the dope man goes." "That's the place where all those poor people go." If that is the worse thing that can be said about our ministry, I believe we are right where the Lord would have us to be. My goal is to raise up a group of Ananias's who aren't afraid to get their hands dirty. If we can impact our community one Saul at a time, I believe that will give birth to a Paul that may become the next great Apostle.

Which brings me to the Timothy tie-in. The reason Paul had to reach back and be a mentor, is because somebody did it for him. Where would Paul be had it not been for Ananias? And none of us would be where we are had someone not taken the time to reach us when we were rough around the edges.

It's very similar to what happened during the Underground Railroad experience. There were men and women who made it to the North to freedom. But they went right back to the South, put their own lives in danger, in order to set their brothers and sisters free. That's what Ananias did for Saul. And that's what Saul/Paul did for Timothy and so many others.

If the Lord has been good to you, you have to come right back and be good to others. Timothy was already religious. But he needed a relationship that would propel him into his destiny. I was already religious when I arrived in Atlanta. But my pastor committed himself to minister to my need a critical time in my development.

You are blessed to be a blessing. We must be compassionate enough to reach back and get someone off their Damascus road. I preach in the prisons because it could have been me in prison. They may be there because they did wrong. But I'm certainly not free because I did right! I taught school because struggled in school. Who better to educate young minds than a person who knows the frustrations of failure?

Investing in Timothy is not just a matter of keeping the business of Church in operation. This was a mandate from heaven to sow back into his community. Understand that this Ananias and Paul model is not just for ministers or pastors. Anyone who has been blessed by God can reach back and bring others along.

The drug dealers in my community are not always quick to hear me. They respect me by virtue of my position. But in their minds I lack credibility because I've never dealt drugs. I don't know their struggle. But do you know who does? All of the former drug dealers who are now members of our church. I commission them to go right back and get some of their friends who still live tat life. If a former gang member, a former kingpin can go out and tell his brothers how Jesus saved him, his testimony alone is enough to save a neighborhood!

The leader of our parking lot ministry, is a former dealer and gang member. He is now married with children, and recently graduated with a Psychology degree from Florida State University. Let me be the first to say the name Brian Stringer. You'll hear more from him in future!

There are countless other men I could tell you about. But the common thread in all of their lives is that they were helped. And now they help others. One of the reasons I am so passionate about education is because I struggled in my own studies. I did not have a learning disability. I did not have any behavioral issues. I had that mental and physical disorder called "lazy." And it was during that six-year season of struggle where the men in my life stepped up to hold me accountable. My father, my teachers, my village of mentors. They reached back to help me. Now I've committed my life to helping others.

I believe part of giving back is seeing the potential in others even when they don't see it in themselves. Timothy was not a ready-made pastor or preacher, neither was Saul in the beginning. But they had potential. Their character was a lump of clay waiting to be molded and mentored. I believe God uses the people in our lives to help get that job done.

Whether you are dealing with the best and the brightest or the worst of the worst, it is not always apparent what they will be in the future. The best could turn out to be the worst. And the worst, could very well turn out to be the best. Did Barack Hussein Obama's third grade teacher know that he would become president of the United States one day? I doubt it. Not even young Barack himself could have predicted such a historic moment being manifested through him.

This is important to those of us who will be a man for someone else. Loving people means being willing to care for them in spite of their condition. They may be resistant like the demon possessed man. And in other cases, it may not be popular to stand behind them in support. This is what I meant when we discussed the ability to meet people where they are.

In most churches, there is a common agreement we share in principal when it comes to hurting people. We care for the families of those whose family members are murdered. We care for those who have been affected by crime in their communities. We embrace those who are victims in some way, shape, or form. But what about the perpetuators of such acts? Who reaches out to them? Who embraces them? Are they not worthy of a mentor or at least a compassionate ear to listen?

I am not saying this is an easy question to answer. In theory we would like to believe that we can reach out and help anybody. But think about what I am suggesting, in real time. Think about what God is commanding us to do. He wants us to mourn with the family of Treyvon Martin, and also seek to restore George Zimmerman.

Yes, God expects us to embrace the family of every victim of the September 11th attacks, but also seek to reconcile our differences with the ones who committed such a heinous act. Being a man for someone is just that extreme. Can you attempt to restore the dope dealer, the child molester, the wife abuser, or a murderer like Saul? Scripture sums it up best when Paul wrote in Ephesians 4:32, "Be ye kind one to another, tenderhearted, forgiving one another, even as God for Christ's sake hath forgiven you."

When we embrace this commandment, we could very well be empowering the next president. But even if he or she doesn't become president, God sees them as being worth the investment. Give back!

QUESTIONS FOR DISCUSSION

1. Have you ever felt judged by others for your mistakes in life? _____

_____

_____

_____

2. Name a person who was able to care for you in spite of your challenges.

_____

_____

_____

3. How did you respond to correction when it was first offered? _____

_____

_____

_____

4. Is there currently a person you are struggling to love or forgive? If so, why? _____

_____

_____

_____

5. What is the risk in reaching out to a man like Saul?_____

_____

_____

_____

_____

CHAPTER 11

Reaching and Teaching

By now we should have a clearer understanding of what it means to have a man or be a man for someone else. But I want to expound on a few more principles in greater detail in order to help you see how this looks in your daily experiences. In other words, how do I go about finding a man if I need one? And how does that dynamic play out in my daily life? Let's look at the three expressions of male mentoring. We have "Reaching Up," "Reaching Out," and "Reaching Down."

Reaching up is all about finding someone who has already been where you are trying to go. These are true mentors. These are the people you can identify based on their experience, their wisdom, and their willingness to be honest about the mistakes they've made along the way.

When you reach up to someone, you understand that they've been where you are trying to go. In most cases they are older than you. But that is not a requirement for becoming your mentor. There are people who occupy the same office that you wish to hold, or someone who has already held the office, successfully or not. When you reach up to a person, you must understand that their mistakes don't disqualify them from helping you. In fact, their mistakes may be the very life lesson you need to know about in order to succeed.

Now that I am an adult, my father has shared many stories and anecdotes with me about his life. He has over 50 years of pastoral experience, but almost 70 years as a man! That's somebody I can listen to. He is very candid with me about his blessings and his lessons. He encourages me just by being honest. Is there anyone in your life that you look up to? It may not be in your immediate family circle. But God will always place people in your path that you can learn from.

Reach up to people in order to gain wisdom. I cannot stress to you enough how important this is. When I reach up to a successful person, or a person who I believe can mentor me, I am not inquiring about the brand of suits he wears. I am not concerned with the kind of car he drives. I'm not concerned with whether or not he can get me into the room with some famous people. Those things are HIS earnings. As a man reaching up to a man, I don't want what he's earned, I want what he's learned.

In my experience, I have been blessed to be in the company of some pretty heavy dudes. Some are millionaires, some are toting the line of poverty. But none of that matters to me. My question to them are always about the journey, the process, the lessons learned on the road to destiny. These are the things you should focus on then reaching up to a person.

When reaching for a mentor, be careful not to limit your reach to a certain demographic. Even people who are different than you can help guide you toward greatness. Black men can't be afraid to talk to White men. White men can't feel it beneath them to learn from Black men. Every race, religion, and even gender can benefit from the wisdom of one person to another.

"Reaching Out" involves the people in your peer group. These are your good friends, your best buddies, and the people who are, for lack of a better term "on your level." I have about three of four men who are close to my age that I would consider to be friends and "reach-out buddies." They struggle with some of the same issues I do. And most times we find ourselves striving toward the same goals. But the difference between the reach-out and the reach-up is that my reach-out men are here for support more than anything.

These are like brothers or sisters compared to your parents. You don't vent your frustrations the same way when you're talking to your parent figures. Your approach is different. And most times, you're more honest with your buddies because they're in no position to judge you.

Every man needs someone in your peer group that you can reach out to. Maybe it's a co-worker, or someone who works in a similar field. For example, LeBron James would reach out to Dwyane Wade as a friend and a brother. But when it's time to reach up, he would go to Bill Russel or any of the other legends of the game. The both have basketball knowledge. But the dynamic of the interaction is different between the reach-up and the reach-out.

Who do you reach out to when you are frustrated with life's

issues? Who can you vent to without the fear of judgement or betrayal? Every man needs a man in his life for this purpose. There are some of you who, like me, don't have many friends. While it is understandable to keep your circle of friends small, you would do well to surround yourself with a few good men who you share common interests with. Married men need the fellowship of other married men. There is a certain perspective you can gain from them. You have that in common. Most single men can't offer you that.

The men you reach out to, they are your teammates. They are not your coaches, because they're struggling on the court just like you. They are trying to figure out the game of life and win just like you. As cool and hip as I believe I am, I understand that my son needs boys his age (who have good sense) to reach out to.

I can remember my friends and I growing up together. We probably came up with some of the craziest ideas about life and how to live it. But the joy is that we had each other for the journey. Every man should have other men around to keep you encouraged and to keep your life in perspective. My friends want nothing for me other than my happiness and success. They want me to be a responsible, accountable vessel for God to use. They don't even care to be mentioned in this book. They are simply happy for the fact that I finally wrote it.

Reaching out and reaching up are equally necessary. One man pushes you forward, and the other man pulls you up. The wiser man reminds you that you can overcome anything, because he did. The older man encourages you to do better than he did. Your peers keep you grounded and prevent you from getting too full of yourself. They know your nickname. They know what you did that Friday night at (you name the place). But they still love you. They don't encourage your foolishness. But they understand you and are willing to pray you through it. You will be this person for them as well.

The last expression of make mentoring involves reaching down which we covered in great detail in the last chapter. You owe it to future generations to reach down and help them along. There may be a man reading this book who had no one to reach down to you. That is the more reason why you should become a mentor.

You remember how hard it was for you as a young man. You remember how angry it made you not having a father figure. That feeling of emptiness and struggle should cause you to reach down to someone. This will not always be a person that you identify as needy. Most times the person you are supposed to mentor will find *you*. They choose you when you weren't even looking to be chosen. That is the best compliment a person can ever pay to your character.

For a young man to want to be like you, for a young adult male to want to spend time around you, for a seasoned man to admit that he needs to be mentored to, that in and of itself is the reason why you should never ignore a person who reaches out to you.

I hear what you are saying to me as you read. Simmons, you can't be everything to everybody. And who has time to be Superman to all these needy people? Well, in theory you are correct. But my advice to you would be to simply make yourself available. Be available when your brother needs advice. Be available when a person needs a hand up. Be more transparent when it comes to your struggles and your mistakes in life. One of the reasons I hesitated, maybe even stalled, to write this book is because of my fear of being critiqued or judged. But when I thought about the many men who God would place in this book's path, I could no longer let fear be a factor in my life. I might be a man for someone I've never even met. And I encourage you to reach on all three levels.

QUESTIONS FOR
DISCUSSION

1. Who do you look up to as a mentor? _____

_____

_____

_____

2. Who are the people you reach out to when you need strength?

_____

_____

_____

3. Are you currently a mentor to anyone?_____

_____

_____

_____

4. What are the struggles of being a mentor? _____

_____

_____

_____

5. Why do some men find it easier to seek help from women rather than men? _____

_____

_____

_____

CHAPTER 12

No More Excuses

As we make our way toward a strong finish, I can hear the cries of many men who are reading this book. Your cries are not those of thanksgiving, but of frustration. As good as all this information is in principle, many of you are still struggling with a lot of this content. Not because you disagree. Many of you are struggling with the fact that "I don't have a man, and can't find a man."

We've already gone through the statistics. And the effects of "manlessness" is apparent in communities all over this world. However, it would encourage us to know that these situations are not unique. But most importantly, they are not hopeless.

Jesus encountered a man one day who was sick for 38 years. In fact, he was sitting in an area where sick people gathered daily, hoping for a miracle. John chapter 5 reveals that they were blind, lame, and paralyzed, waiting for a healing season to occur. In short, there was a pool of water where they laid every day. And there would come a time when an angel would stir the water. And whoever got in the water first, they would be delivered from their physical affliction.

Well, as the story goes, this one man was approached by Jesus. And when He asked the man about his condition and why he had been there so long, he replied "I have no man to put me in the water. And whenever I would get in myself, someone else jumps in ahead of me." That's a tough situation for a man trying to get better in life.

That brings me to the discouraged person reading this book. What can we say to the brother who had no man to show him how to be a man? You had no one to mentor you. You had no example of what godly manhood is all about. You may be like my students who were the man of their house at 12-years-old. What do we say to the man who had no man?

To you I say, "no more excuses!" It is easy to use our lack of examples as an excuse for why we are in bad moral shape. Many men will testify that not having a father figure brought more pain and dysfunction to their lives. Many females will confess that a lack of male involvement has hurt them and their future possibilities. But while all of these statistics may ring true, the fact still remains that not having a man is no excuse in the sight of God.

Jesus asked the paralyzed man a simple question. Do you want to be made whole? It sounds simple enough. But that is question we must all answer. Do you want to be a good husband? Do you want to be a functional father? Do you want to have healthy relationships and make better choices? If so, there is hope for you.

God is offering you the opportunity to do what has never been done for you. And a chance to have what you thought was impossible. All the scars from your past hurts can be healed. All the dysfunction and disarray can be fixed through the filter of your faith. All you have to do is take up your bed and walk.

In other words, the very thing you've been laying on as an excuse, you have to be willing to pick that thing up and carry it as a testimony. The fact that you didn't have a father is the reason why you should seek to be a better father. Your prayer from this point on is for the Lord to place a man in your path who can help you understand your past, filter it, forgive it, and function in spite of it.

It is never too late for you to make a fresh start. You cannot spend the rest of your life with a raggedy beard simply because you never had a man to teach you how to shave. Today is a new opportunity. And there is no mistake or misfortune that you can't overcome with Christ on your side.

If the men in your life were abusive, let that be an example of what not to do. But not an excuse for you to repeat the sin. If the men in your life were irresponsible and unaccountable, let that be a warning sign for you to go in a different direction. There are millions of men like you who have struggled through some of the same issues. But the difference is they made up their mind to get up and do something about it.

Please know that I am not minimizing your struggle. But the excuses we make as men are not acceptable to the God who made us. Where there's a will, there's a way. And if you want to be made whole, there's a man named Jesus who can help you get there.

Often times, when we're crafting programs and developing ministries to help people in need, we forget the very One who gives us power to pull it off. When Jesus told that paralyzed man to take up his bed and walk, He said it with full intentions to help him do it. To the brother who says you don't have a man, we just took away all your excuses. Jesus is your man!

All you have to do in confess what you are struggling with at the moment, and ask Him to be the man and the Master of your life. What's more important than your physical and emotional infirmity is the sin that is holding you back from God's intended plan for your life. His objective is not just to heal you, but to save you, The fact that you didn't have a father who was a preacher or a brother who made all the right choices, there is no reason why you can't be the first in your circle to be made whole.

My brother, you can be the Paul who brings millions of others to Christ. You can be the David who bounces back from the pit of shame and despair. You can be the father of the century even if your father never gave you a day of his time. Don't let their failures be your funeral. Use it as motivation to get right with God and do it now!

One thing we know for sure is that you can't accomplish anything on your own. I am not telling you to simply be a man. I'm telling you to get in touch with the Man who is above every other man. There is a greater man than your father who wasn't there. There is a greater man than they men who set a bad example for you. There is a more powerful man than the ones who took so much from you. All you have to do in accept Him as your Savior and connect with a group of believers who will help you in this journey. He is the ultimate Man for us, and He will use other men to mentor you along the way.

To the man who is reading this in your prison cell, you have no excuse. To the man who is struggling with addiction, you have no excuse. To the man who is wondering whether you can recover from decades of demons and dysfunction, today is the first day to your recovery. It's time for you to walk in the assignment that God has purposed for you!

QUESTIONS FOR DISCUSSION

1. What excuses do we often hear from men about their problems in life?

_____

_____

_____

2. Are these excuses legitimate in most cases?_____

_____

_____

_____

3. What would you say to a friend who has been facing difficult life issues for an extended period of time? _____

_____

_____

_____

4. How have you used you own struggles to minister to someone else?

_____

_____

_____

Closing Thoughts

My prayer is that you were encouraged by the words you have read. This book should serve as a guide for men's ministry groups, mentoring initiatives, and even women's discussion groups from time to time. Sports teams should read this book. College students should gather in groups and discuss what you've read. Your biggest struggle may be finding a man to reach out to. As men we are very private, almost to the point of defensiveness when it comes to our needs and our weaknesses.

Again I want to thank the men in my life who have given me the courage to write and reach others. In order to make sure we've covered all our bases, let's use these 10 items as a checklist for how to implement these ideas in real-time.

1. Familiarize yourself with what God says about manhood.
2. Connect with a Bible-based church/ministry that meets your needs as a man.

3. Pray daily about the issues you struggle with.

4. Look for a man to reach up to who is more seasoned than you.

5. Look for a man to reach out to within your peer group.

6. Be on the lookout for people who may be reaching up to you as a guide.

7. Work with a school in your community to become an official mentor for a young person.

8. Support ministries and community efforts that serve struggling men.

9. Make every effort to maintain a healthy relationship with your children.

10. Feed your relationship with Christ by attending worship, Bible study, and serving in ministry outreach and activities.

Need additional copies?

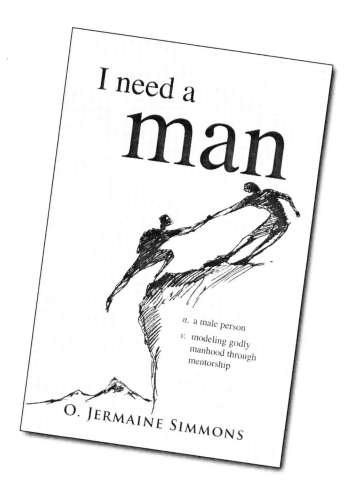

To order more copies,
contact CertaPublishing.com

❐   Order online at:
CertaPublishing.com/INeedAMan

❐   Call 855-77-CERTA or

❐   Email Info@CertaPublishing.com